Table of Contents

- Overview of Different Investment Options (Stocks, Bonds, Real Estate, etc.)

- Pros and Cons of Each Investment Type

Building an Investment Portfolio

- Asset Allocation Strategies

- Portfolio Rebalancing Techniques

Evaluating Investment Opportunities

- Fundamental Analysis

- Technical Analysis

Market Trends and Economic Factors

- Understanding Market Cycles

- Economic Indicators and their Impact on Investments

Ethics and Social Responsibility in Investing

- Responsible Investment Practices

- Impact Investing

Tax Planning and Optimization

- Tax-Efficient Investing Strategies

- Importance of Tax Planning in Investments

Retirement Planning

Introduction

In a world where financial security and independence have become increasingly crucial, the journey towards becoming a money-minded investor holds unparalleled significance. The essence of financial independence lies not just in earning money but in making it work for you—through investing. However, the realm of investments can seem daunting and complex, deterring many from taking their initial steps. Yet, with a systematic approach and a clear roadmap, even novices can embark on this transformative journey toward financial empowerment.

Understanding the Money-Minded Investor:

At its core, a money-minded investor is someone who recognizes the value of their hard-earned money and endeavors to make it grow. This mindset transcends merely saving for a rainy day; it's about leveraging opportunities to generate wealth and secure a stable financial future. However, the first hurdle often encountered is the lack of knowledge and confidence in navigating the intricate landscape of investments.

The Importance of Investing:

Investing serves as the cornerstone of financial stability and growth. It transcends the limitations of mere saving by putting money to work and allowing it to multiply over time. Whether aiming for retirement security, building wealth, or achieving specific financial goals, investing offers the means to attain these aspirations. However, the prospect of venturing into this realm might seem daunting, riddled with uncertainties and risks.

Overcoming the Barriers:

For many potential investors, fear and uncertainty form significant barriers to entry into the world of investments. The fear of losing hard-earned money, coupled with the perceived complexity of investment avenues, often results in hesitation. However, it's imperative to acknowledge that with the right knowledge, strategy, and a disciplined approach, the risks can be mitigated.

Simple, Smart Steps to Start Investing:

The path to becoming a money-minded investor commences with understanding the basics. It involves acquainting oneself with different investment vehicles, risk profiles, and aligning investment choices with personal financial goals. Diving headfirst into intricate financial jargon may seem intimidating, but starting with the fundamentals lays a sturdy foundation.

Establishing Financial Goals:

Before embarking on any investment journey, defining clear and achievable financial goals is paramount. Whether aiming for short-term gains, long-term wealth accumulation, or specific milestones like buying a house or funding education, setting realistic targets serves as a guiding light.

Educating Yourself:

Knowledge is the most potent tool in an investor's arsenal. Learning about various investment options, risk tolerance, market trends, and the power of compounding interest empowers individuals to make informed decisions. Numerous resources, from books to online courses and seminars, cater to both beginners and seasoned investors seeking to broaden their financial acumen.

Building a Diversified Portfolio:

Diversification is a key strategy to mitigate risk. Spreading investments across different asset classes, such as stocks, bonds, real estate, and mutual funds, helps cushion against market volatility. It's crucial to strike a balance between potential returns and risk tolerance while building a diversified portfolio.

Embracing a Long-Term Approach:

Patience is a virtue in investing. While market fluctuations might induce short-term panic, adopting a long-term perspective is essential. Time in the market often outweighs timing the market, emphasizing the significance of staying invested through market cycles to realize compounding gains.

Seeking Professional Advice:

For those feeling overwhelmed or unsure about their investment decisions, seeking guidance from financial advisors or planners can be immensely beneficial. These professionals can provide personalized advice based on individual financial circumstances and goals.

The Roadmap to Financial Independence:

Becoming a money-minded investor doesn't merely entail making random investments. It involves creating a comprehensive roadmap tailored to achieve financial independence.

Setting Milestones:

Breaking down overarching financial goals into achievable milestones ensures steady progress. It allows for regular assessment and recalibration of strategies to stay on track.

Consistent Monitoring and Adjustments:

Regularly reviewing and adjusting the investment portfolio in response to changing market conditions or life circumstances is crucial. Rebalancing the portfolio and making necessary adjustments helps maintain alignment with financial objectives.

Continual Learning and Adaptation:

The financial landscape is dynamic, with constant changes in regulations, market trends, and economic conditions. Thus, an investor's journey towards financial independence necessitates a commitment to lifelong learning and adaptability.

CHAPTER 1

Understanding the Money-Minded Investor

Investing is a multifaceted activity, shaped by various approaches, mindsets, and goals. One such approach is that of the money-minded investor, whose primary focus revolves around financial gains and wealth accumulation. Understanding the characteristics, traits, and underlying principles of a money-minded investor is crucial in comprehending their investment strategies and motivations.

- **Defining a Money-Minded Investor**

A money-minded investor can be defined as an individual whose primary objective in investing is to maximize financial returns and wealth accumulation. This investor is primarily focused on profit generation, driven by financial metrics, such as ROI (Return on Investment), profitability ratios, and wealth growth. Their investment decisions are predominantly guided by the potential for monetary gain rather than other factors, such as social impact, personal values, or emotional attachment.

Money-minded investors often adopt a pragmatic and analytical approach to their investment decisions. They meticulously analyze market trends, financial statements, economic indicators, and other quantitative data to make informed investment choices. They tend to prioritize risk management and seek opportunities that offer the highest potential for returns within their risk tolerance levels.

- **Characteristics and Traits**

1. **Financially Goal-Oriented:**

Money-minded investors are driven by clear financial goals. These goals might include retirement planning, wealth accumulation, funding education or achieving specific financial milestones. They meticulously craft strategies aligning with these objectives.

2. **Risk-Awareness and Management:**

They understand and manage risk effectively. While seeking high returns, they balance their risk exposure, diversify their portfolio, and undertake calculated risks.

3. **Research-Oriented:**

Thorough research is a hallmark of money-minded investors. They dedicate considerable time and effort to analyzing market trends, company financials, and economic indicators. They make informed decisions based on comprehensive research.

4. **Profit Maximization:**

Their primary focus is on maximizing profits. They seek investments with the potential for high returns and constantly reassess their portfolio to optimize gains.

5. **Long-Term Vision:**

Money-minded investors often have a long-term perspective. They understand the power of compounding and are patient in their investment approach, willing to wait for the right opportunities to yield significant returns.

6. **Adaptability and Learning:**

They stay updated with market changes, technological advancements, and economic shifts. They adapt their strategies accordingly and are open to learning from both successes and failures.

7. **Discipline and Patience:**

These investors exhibit discipline in adhering to their investment strategies and exercise patience, avoiding impulsive decisions driven by market volatility or short-term fluctuations.

8. **Objective-Oriented Decision Making:**

They make decisions based on objective analysis rather than emotions or hearsay. Their choices are grounded in data and informed evaluations.

9. **Focus on Asset Allocation:**

Money-minded investors understand the significance of asset allocation in risk management. They diversify their investments across various asset classes to spread risk effectively.

10. **Continuous Evaluation and Adjustment:**

They continuously evaluate their investment portfolio, adjusting it as per market conditions, performance metrics, and changes in personal financial goals.

Conclusion

Understanding the mindset, behaviors, and priorities of a money-minded investor offers valuable insights into their approach to investing. While their primary focus is on financial gains, their strategies, discipline, and long-term vision often contribute to building wealth steadily over time. Balancing risk with reward, meticulous research, and a commitment to financial goals characterize these investors, making them a distinct and vital segment of the investment landscape.

CHAPTER 2

Psychology and Mindset of Money-Minded Investors

In the world of finance, success in investing isn't just about numbers and strategies; it heavily relies on the psychology and mindset of the investor. The mindset of money-minded investors plays a pivotal role in their decision-making process, risk tolerance, and overall success in the financial markets. Understanding the psychological aspects and overcoming barriers is crucial for navigating the complex landscape of investing.

- **The Role of Mindset in Investing**

a. Rationality vs. Emotionality:

Investing is often perceived as a rational, numbers-driven activity. However, emotions play a significant role. The interplay between fear, greed, and confidence can heavily influence investment decisions. Rational investors strive to make decisions based on data and analysis, but emotions can cloud judgment and lead to impulsive actions.

b. Long-term vs. Short-term Perspective:

Money-minded investors often prioritize a long-term view over short-term gains. They understand the power of compounding and are willing to endure short-term fluctuations for long-term growth. This mindset enables them to stay focused on their investment goals despite market volatility.

c. Risk Perception and Risk Tolerance:

Every investor has a unique perception of risk. Money-minded investors assess risks objectively and understand that all investments carry some level of risk. They determine their risk tolerance by considering their financial goals, time horizon, and personal comfort with volatility. This mindset allows them to take calculated risks aligned with their objectives.

d. Continuous Learning and Adaptability:

Successful investors embrace a growth mindset, acknowledging that the financial landscape is constantly evolving. They are open to learning from both successes and failures, adapting their strategies based on new information and market dynamics. This flexibility enables them to navigate changing market conditions effectively.

- **Overcoming Psychological Barriers**

a. Cognitive Biases:

Investors are susceptible to various cognitive biases that can hinder rational decision-making. For instance, confirmation bias leads investors to seek information that confirms their existing beliefs while ignoring contradictory evidence. Overcoming these biases requires conscious effort, critical thinking, and seeking diverse perspectives.

b. Fear and Greed:

Fear of losses and the desire for quick gains often drive irrational investment decisions. Money-minded investors recognize these emotions and employ strategies to mitigate their impact. They set realistic expectations, diversify their portfolios, and practice disciplined investment approaches to counteract impulsive behaviors.

c. Patience and Discipline:

Patience is a virtue in investing, yet many struggle to remain patient during market fluctuations. Money-minded investors cultivate discipline by sticking to their investment plans, avoiding knee-jerk reactions to market noise, and focusing on long-term objectives rather than short-term fluctuations.

d. Seeking Professional Guidance:

Acknowledging one's limitations and seeking advice from financial professionals can be instrumental in overcoming psychological barriers. Financial advisors provide objective insights, help in crafting a well-thought-out investment strategy, and offer emotional support during turbulent market conditions.

In conclusion, the psychology and mindset of money-minded investors significantly influence their investment journey. Developing a rational, long-term perspective, overcoming psychological barriers, and continuously learning are key elements that shape successful investors. By understanding these psychological aspects and employing strategies to navigate them, investors can enhance their decision-making processes and increase their chances of achieving their financial goals.

CHAPTER 3

Financial Literacy and Education

Financial literacy refers to the knowledge and skills required to make informed and effective decisions about money management. It involves understanding various financial aspects such as budgeting, investing, debt management, and financial planning. In today's complex economic landscape, possessing financial literacy is paramount for individuals and communities alike.

- **Importance of Financial Literacy**

Empowerment through Knowledge

Financial literacy empowers individuals to take control of their finances. It equips them with the understanding needed to navigate the intricacies of personal finance, enabling better decision-making and long-term financial stability.

Mitigating Financial Risks

A lack of financial literacy often leads to poor financial decisions, accumulating debt, falling victim to scams, or not planning for retirement. By contrast, being financially literate helps mitigate these risks, fostering economic resilience against unforeseen challenges.

Socio Economic Impact

On a broader scale, improving financial literacy positively impacts communities and nations. It contributes to economic growth by fostering a financially savvy populace that makes sound financial choices, thereby strengthening the economy.

Education and Access

Access to financial education is a crucial component of financial literacy. By imparting knowledge and skills from an early age, educational institutions play a pivotal role in shaping responsible financial behavior and creating a foundation for lifelong learning.

- **Strategies for Continuous Learning**

Utilizing Online Resources

The digital age offers a plethora of resources for continuous learning. Websites, apps, and online courses provide accessible and often free or affordable avenues to expand financial knowledge. Platforms like Khan Academy, Investopedia, and Coursera offer courses on various financial topics.

Seeking Professional Guidance

Financial advisors and planners can provide personalized guidance based on individual circumstances. Engaging with these professionals allows for tailored financial strategies and insights into complex financial matters.

Reading and Research

Books, articles, and reputable financial publications remain invaluable resources. Classics like "Rich Dad Poor Dad" by Robert Kiyosaki or "The Intelligent Investor" by Benjamin Graham offer timeless insights, while staying updated with current financial news and trends is equally important.

Participating in Workshops and Seminars

Attending workshops and seminars conducted by financial experts provides interactive learning experiences. These events often cover specific financial topics in-depth, allowing participants to engage, ask questions, and gain practical insights.

Engaging in Practical Application

Applying financial knowledge in real-life scenarios reinforces learning. Activities such as budgeting, investing in stocks or mutual funds, and managing debt firsthand contribute significantly to improving financial literacy.

Collaborative Learning and Discussion

Participating in financial discussion groups, forums, or clubs fosters a collaborative learning environment. Sharing experiences, asking questions, and learning from others' perspectives enhances understanding and promotes continuous learning.

Conclusion

Financial literacy is a crucial skill in today's world. It empowers individuals, mitigates risks, and positively impacts societies and economies. Continuous learning through various strategies ensures that individuals stay abreast of evolving financial landscapes, enabling them to make informed and prudent financial decisions.

CHAPTER 4

Setting Financial Goals

Financial goals serve as guiding principles that help individuals manage their finances effectively, ensuring a secure future. They provide direction, motivation, and a framework for making financial decisions. In this comprehensive guide, we'll delve into the significance of setting financial goals, distinguish between short-term and long-term goals, and outline a roadmap for achieving financial success.

Setting Financial Goals:

Importance of Setting Financial Goals:

- Establishing clear financial goals is crucial for creating a roadmap towards financial stability and success.

- Goals act as benchmarks to measure progress, enhance financial discipline, and foster better money management habits.

Types of Financial Goals:

a. Short-Term Goals:

- Short-term goals typically span up to one year and focus on immediate expenses or objectives.

- Examples include building an emergency fund, paying off credit card debt, or saving for a vacation.

b. Long-Term Goals:

- Long-term goals extend beyond five years and often involve significant milestones like retirement planning, buying a home, or funding education.

- They require consistent effort and strategic planning to achieve.

Defining Short-Term and Long-Term Goals:

Short-Term Goals:

- Short-term goals are specific, achievable objectives set within a shorter timeframe.

- They are instrumental in managing immediate financial obligations and addressing pressing needs.

- Examples of short-term goals encompass creating a budget, clearing high-interest debts, or saving for a down payment.

Long-Term Goals:

- Long-term goals encompass broader aspirations that necessitate planning and sustained effort over an extended period.

- These goals often revolve around major life events such as retirement, purchasing a house, or funding children's education.

- They require consistent saving, investing, and periodic reassessment to align with evolving circumstances.

Creating a Roadmap for Financial Success:

Assessing Current Financial Situation:

- Evaluate income, expenses, assets, and liabilities to gain a comprehensive understanding of your financial standing.

- Identify areas for improvement and establish a baseline for setting realistic goals.

SMART Goal Setting:

- Set Specific, Measurable, Achievable, Relevant, and Time-bound (SMART) goals.

- Specific: Define clear and precise objectives.

- Measurable: Establish criteria to track progress.

- Achievable: Set realistic goals considering available resources.

- Relevant: Ensure goals align with your financial priorities.

- Time-bound: Set deadlines to create a sense of urgency.

Prioritizing Goals:

- Prioritize goals based on urgency, importance, and impact on your financial well-being

- Allocate resources and effort accordingly to accomplish each goal effectively.

Creating a Budget:

- Develop a comprehensive budget outlining income, expenses, and savings goals.

- Track spending habits to ensure alignment with financial objectives and identify areas for potential savings.

Implementing Strategies for Goal Achievement:

- Employ strategies like automation of savings, debt repayment plans, diversifying investments, and seeking professional financial advice.

- Regularly review and adjust goals as circumstances change, ensuring continued progress.

Conclusion:

Setting financial goals, whether short-term or long-term, is instrumental in achieving financial stability and securing one's future. By understanding the distinction between these goals, creating a roadmap aligned with SMART principles, and diligently working towards them, individuals can navigate their financial journey effectively. Regular evaluation and adaptation of goals ensure flexibility and sustained progress towards financial success.

CHAPTER 5

Risk Management and Diversification

Risk is an inherent component of any investment or financial endeavor. It represents the potential for an outcome that differs from expectations and can have varying degrees of impact, ranging from negligible to catastrophic. Understanding, assessing, and managing risk is crucial in the world of finance. One of the fundamental strategies employed to handle risk is diversification. This comprehensive guide will delve into the essence of risk management, elucidate the dynamics of risk and its impact, and elucidate strategies for effective diversification.

- **Understanding Risk and Its Impact**

Risk, in financial terms, encapsulates the probability that an investment's actual return will deviate from its expected return. It's a multifaceted concept influenced by various factors, including market volatility, economic instability, geopolitical events, and more. It's vital to recognize that while risk is often associated with negative outcomes, it can also present opportunities for growth and profit.

The impact of risk can be categorized into different types

Market Risk: This type of risk arises due to fluctuations in the market. Factors like interest rates, inflation, and economic conditions affect market risk. For instance, a sudden economic downturn can significantly impact stock prices.

Credit Risk: It pertains to the potential of a borrower failing to meet their debt obligations. Lenders face credit risk when lending funds to individuals or entities. Defaults on loans or bonds are examples of credit risk.

Liquidity Risk: It refers to the possibility of not being able to sell an investment quickly at a fair price. Investments in assets with low liquidity can pose this risk, leading to difficulties in converting them into cash without significant loss.

Operational Risk: This risk is linked to internal processes, systems, or people. It includes risks from inadequate procedures, human errors, technology failures, and fraud. Operational risk can significantly impact an organization's efficiency and financial stability.

The Impact of Risk on Investments

Understanding the impact of risk on investments is crucial. Higher risks often correlate with the potential for higher returns. Investments with higher perceived risks typically offer greater rewards to compensate for the uncertainty involved. However, these investments also have a higher probability of losses.

Risk and Return: The Risk-Return Tradeoff

The relationship between risk and return is a cornerstone of investment theory. It implies that higher potential returns are associated with higher levels of risk. Investors must balance their risk tolerance with their desired return. Investments perceived as low-risk, like government bonds, generally offer lower returns compared to higher-risk investments such as stocks or commodities.

- **Strategies for Diversification**

Diversification is a risk management technique that involves spreading investments across different assets, industries, or geographic regions to reduce exposure to any single asset or risk. It is based on the principle that not all assets react similarly to market changes or economic events.

Asset Allocation: Allocating investments across different asset classes, such as stocks, bonds, real estate, and commodities, helps manage risk. Each asset class behaves differently under various market conditions, reducing overall portfolio volatility.

Diversifying Within Asset Classes: Within each asset class, diversification can further mitigate risk. For instance, within the stock market, diversifying across industries, company sizes, and geographic locations can reduce specific risks associated with any single stock.

Rebalancing: Regularly reviewing and rebalancing a portfolio ensures that it aligns with the investor's risk tolerance and investment goals. Rebalancing involves selling overperforming assets and purchasing underperforming ones to maintain the desired asset allocation.

International Diversification: Investing in assets from different countries or regions can reduce risks associated with a single country's economic or political events. International diversification provides exposure to various markets and currencies, potentially mitigating risks associated with domestic market fluctuations.

Conclusion

Risk management and diversification are integral components of sound financial planning. Understanding the various types of risks and their impact on investments enables investors to make informed decisions. Employing diversification strategies helps spread risk and optimize the risk-return tradeoff. By implementing these strategies, investors can enhance their chances of achieving their financial objectives while minimizing potential losses

CHAPTER 6

Investment Vehicles

Investing is a critical component of financial planning, allowing individuals to grow their wealth and achieve long-term financial goals. With a plethora of investment options available, understanding the characteristics, advantages, and drawbacks of each investment vehicle is crucial for making informed financial decisions. This comprehensive guide provides an overview of different investment options such as stocks, bonds, real estate, and more, outlining their pros and cons.

- **Stocks**

Overview: Stocks represent ownership in a company. When an individual buys shares of a company's stock, they become a partial owner and are entitled to a portion of the company's profits.

Pros:

High Potential Returns: Stocks have historically offered high returns compared to other investment options over the long term.

Liquidity: Stocks are highly liquid investments, enabling investors to buy and sell easily.

Diversification: Investors can diversify their portfolio by investing in various stocks across different industries.

Cons:

Volatility: Stock prices can be highly volatile, leading to fluctuations and potential losses.

Risk of Loss: Investing in individual stocks carries the risk of losing the entire investment if the company performs poorly.

Requires Research: Successful stock investing often requires substantial research and knowledge of the market.

- **Bonds**

Overview: Bonds are debt securities where investors lend money to a government or corporation in exchange for periodic interest payments and the return of the principal amount at maturity.

Pros:

Stability and Income: Bonds generally offer a more stable income stream through regular interest payments.

Preservation of Capital: Bonds are considered less risky than stocks, providing a more secure investment.

Diversification: Including bonds in a portfolio can help balance risk due to their typically lower volatility compared to stocks.

Cons:

Interest Rate Risk: Bond prices can be impacted negatively when interest rates rise, leading to potential losses for bondholders.

Inflation Risk: Inflation can erode the purchasing power of bond returns over time.

Lower Potential Returns: Bonds generally offer lower returns compared to stocks, potentially limiting overall portfolio growth.

- **Real Estate**

Overview: Real estate involves investing in physical properties such as residential homes, commercial buildings, or land with the expectation of generating income or capital appreciation.

Pros:

Steady Income: Real estate investments can provide a steady stream of rental income.

Appreciation: Properties may increase in value over time, offering capital appreciation.

Diversification: Real estate investments can diversify a portfolio, reducing overall risk.

Cons:

Illiquidity: Real estate investments are less liquid compared to stocks and bonds, making it challenging to sell quickly.

High Initial Cost: Acquiring properties often requires a substantial initial investment, limiting entry for some investors.

Maintenance and Management: Property ownership involves maintenance costs and management responsibilities.

- **Mutual Funds**

Overview: Mutual funds pool money from multiple investors to invest in a diversified portfolio of stocks, bonds, or other securities managed by a professional fund manager.

Pros:

Diversification: Mutual funds offer diversification across various assets, reducing individual risk.

Professional Management: Fund managers make investment decisions based on research and expertise.

Accessibility: Mutual funds are accessible to individual investors with varying capital amounts.

Cons:

Fees: Some mutual funds charge management fees and other expenses that can impact overall returns.

Lack of Control: Investors have limited control over specific securities within the fund.

Potential Underperformance: Not all mutual funds outperform the market, and some may underperform due to various factors.

- **Exchange-Traded Funds (ETFs)**

Overview: ETFs are investment funds traded on stock exchanges, mirroring the performance of an underlying index or asset.

Pros:

Diversification: ETFs offer diversification like mutual funds but trade like individual stocks.

Liquidity and Flexibility: ETFs can be bought or sold throughout the trading day at market prices.

Lower Expenses: ETFs generally have lower expense ratios compared to some mutual funds.

Cons:

Brokerage Commissions: Investors may incur brokerage commissions when buying or selling ETF shares.

Tracking Error: Some ETFs may not perfectly track their underlying index, leading to discrepancies in performance.

Potential Volatility: Like stocks, ETF prices can be subject to market volatility.

- **Commodities**

Overview: Commodities include physical goods such as gold, oil, agricultural products, etc., traded on exchanges.

Pros:

Inflation Hedge: Certain commodities, like gold, may act as a hedge against inflation.

Portfolio Diversification: Investing in commodities can diversify a portfolio and reduce overall risk.

Potential for High Returns: Certain commodities can experience significant price increases during supply and demand imbalances.

Cons:

Volatility: Prices of commodities can be highly volatile due to factors like geopolitical events, weather, etc.

Storage and Handling Costs: Holding physical commodities may involve storage and maintenance expenses.

Lack of Income: Unlike stocks or bonds, commodities generally do not generate income through dividends or interest.

Conclusion

Each investment vehicle carries its own set of risks and potential rewards. Understanding the characteristics and considering personal financial goals, risk tolerance, and time horizon are crucial when selecting investment options. Diversification across multiple asset classes often helps mitigate risk and optimize returns in a well-rounded investment portfolio. Investors should conduct thorough research or seek professional advice before making any investment decisions to align with their specific financial objectives and risk tolerance levels.

CHAPTER 7

Building an Investment Portfolio

Investing is a prudent way to grow wealth over time, but success hinges on constructing a well-diversified investment portfolio and maintaining its balance through astute management. Asset allocation strategies and portfolio rebalancing techniques are integral components in achieving long-term investment goals while managing risk. This comprehensive guide will delve into these two pillars of successful investing, offering insights into their significance, various methodologies, and practical application.

- **Asset Allocation Strategies**

1. Understanding Asset Allocation

Asset allocation is the process of dividing an investment portfolio among different asset classes, such as stocks, bonds, real estate, and cash equivalents. Its primary goal is to optimize returns while mitigating risk according to an investor's risk tolerance, time horizon, and financial goals. The classic rule of thumb is to spread investments across various asset classes, reducing the impact of market volatility on the portfolio's overall performance.

2. Types of Asset Classes

- *Equities (Stocks):* Equities represent ownership in a company and offer the potential for high returns but also come with higher volatility.

- *Fixed-Income (Bonds):* Bonds are debt securities issued by governments or corporations, offering regular interest payments and relatively lower risk compared to stocks.

- *Real Estate:* Real estate investments involve purchasing properties or real estate investment trusts (REITs) that can generate rental income or capital appreciation.

- *Cash and Cash Equivalents:* These include savings accounts, certificates of deposit (CDs), and Treasury bills, providing stability and liquidity to a portfolio.

3. Asset Allocation Models

- *Strategic Asset Allocation:* This approach sets fixed percentages for different asset classes based on long-term objectives and risk tolerance.

- *Tactical Asset Allocation:* This strategy involves adjusting the portfolio's allocation based on short-term market opportunities or changing economic conditions.

- *Dynamic Asset Allocation:* Utilizing a mix of both strategic and tactical approaches, this method adapts the portfolio's allocation in response to market fluctuations while maintaining a long-term strategy.

4. Factors Influencing Asset Allocation

- *Investor's Age and Time Horizon:* Younger investors with longer time horizons may favor more aggressive allocations, while older investors might opt for a more conservative approach.

- *Risk Tolerance:* Investors with a higher risk tolerance may allocate more to equities, seeking higher returns despite increased volatility.

- *Market Conditions:* Economic cycles, interest rates, and geopolitical events can influence the performance of different asset classes, prompting adjustments in asset allocation.

- **Portfolio Rebalancing Techniques**

1. Importance of Portfolio Rebalancing

Portfolio rebalancing is the process of realigning the portfolio's asset allocation back to its original or desired target allocation. Over time, the market's fluctuations can cause asset classes to deviate from their intended percentages, leading to increased risk or suboptimal returns. Re-balancing helps maintain the desired risk-return profile.

2. Re-balancing Strategies

- *Calendar-Based Re-balancing:* Investors set specific time intervals (quarterly, annually) to rebalance their portfolios regardless of market conditions.

- *Threshold-Based Re-balancing:* This method involves re-balancing when an asset class deviates from its target allocation by a predetermined percentage (e.g., 5%).

- *Cash Flow Re-balancing:* Re-balancing is done when adding new funds or withdrawing from the portfolio, ensuring that new investments align with the target allocation.

3. Methods of Re-balancing

- *Sell-High, Buy-Low Approach:* Re-balancing involves selling over-performing assets and buying underperforming assets to maintain the desired allocation.

- *Contribution Re-balancing:* New contributions are allocated to asset classes that are underrepresented in the portfolio, helping to re-balance over time without selling existing assets.

4. Considerations for Effective Re-balancing

- *Transaction Costs:* Re-balancing may incur transaction fees or tax implications, influencing the frequency and method of re-balancing.

- *Tax Efficiency:* Utilizing tax-advantaged accounts and considering tax consequences while re-balancing can optimize after-tax returns.

Conclusion

Constructing an investment portfolio with a well-thought-out asset allocation strategy and implementing effective portfolio rebalancing techniques are crucial for long-term investment success. Investors should periodically review their portfolios, considering changing goals, market conditions, and risk tolerance, to ensure that their investments remain aligned with their objectives. By employing prudent asset allocation and disciplined portfolio rebalancing, investors can navigate market fluctuations while striving for consistent growth and risk management in their investment journey.

CHAPTER 8

Evaluating Investment Opportunities

Investing in financial markets involves assessing various investment opportunities to make informed decisions that can yield profitable returns. Two primary methods used by investors to evaluate investment opportunities are Fundamental Analysis and Technical Analysis. These approaches are distinct in their methodologies, tools, and perspectives but are both valuable in providing insights into potential investments.

- **Fundamental Analysis**

Understanding Fundamental Analysis

Fundamental analysis involves evaluating a company's intrinsic value by examining its financial statements, economic indicators, industry trends, and qualitative aspects such as management quality and competitive advantages. The goal is to determine whether the current market price accurately reflects the true value of the asset.

Key Components of Fundamental Analysis

Financial Statements Analysis

- *Income Statement:* Evaluating revenues, expenses, and profits over a specific period to assess the company's profitability.

- *Balance Sheet:* Reviewing assets, liabilities, and equity to understand the company's financial health and leverage.

- *Cash Flow Statement:* Analyzing cash inflows and outflows to assess the company's ability to generate cash.

Economic Indicators and Industry Analysis

- *Macroeconomic Factors:* Considering interest rates, inflation, GDP growth, and other economic indicators influencing the market.

- *Industry Trends:* Understanding the industry's growth prospects, competitive landscape, and regulatory environment.

Qualitative Factors

- *Management Quality:* Assessing the leadership's competency, transparency, and strategic decision-making.

- *Competitive Advantages:* Identifying unique strengths like brand loyalty, patents, or technological advancements.

Pros and Cons of Fundamental Analysis

Pros

- Provides a comprehensive understanding of a company's financial health and growth potential.

- Long-term oriented and suitable for value investing strategies.

- Consider qualitative aspects that may not be reflected in market prices.

Cons

- Time-consuming due to the extensive research required.

- Subjective nature of qualitative assessments.

- Doesn't account for short-term market fluctuations or investor sentiment.

- **Technical Analysis**

Understanding Technical Analysis

Technical analysis focuses on analyzing historical market data, primarily price and volume, to forecast future price movements. It revolves around the belief that historical price trends and patterns repeat themselves and can predict future market movements.

Key Components of Technical Analysis

Price Charts and Patterns

- *Support and Resistance Levels:* Identifying price levels where the asset tends to stop or reverse.

- *Trend Lines:* Recognizing patterns indicating the direction of the market.

- *Chart Patterns:* Analyzing formations like head and shoulders, triangles, or flags to predict price movements.

Technical Indicators

- *Moving Averages:* Assessing trends by smoothing out price fluctuations.

- *Relative Strength Index (RSI):* Measuring overbought or oversold conditions.

- *MACD (Moving Average Convergence Divergence):* Indicating changes in momentum.

Pros and Cons of Technical Analysis

Pros

- Focuses on short-term price movements and market sentiment.

- Provides clear entry and exit points for trades.

- Works well in liquid markets where price trends are more pronounced.

Cons

- Relies heavily on historical data, which may not predict future market behavior accurately.

- Ignore fundamental factors influencing asset value.

- Interpretation of patterns and indicators can be subjective.

Conclusion

Fundamental analysis and technical analysis offer distinct approaches to evaluating investment opportunities, each with its strengths and limitations. While fundamental analysis delves deep into a company's financials and qualitative factors to determine its intrinsic value, technical analysis focuses on price patterns and market trends to predict short-term price movements.

Successful investors often use a combination of both approaches, known as a "hybrid" or "balanced" approach, to mitigate the weaknesses of each method. They leverage fundamental analysis to identify promising assets based on their long-term potential and use technical analysis to time their entries and exits in the market.

Ultimately, the choice between fundamental and technical analysis depends on an investor's preferences, investment horizon, risk tolerance, and the specific asset being evaluated. Adapting a flexible approach that incorporates elements from both methodologies can enhance the overall investment decision-making process and improve the likelihood of making profitable investment choices.

In conclusion, whether an investor favors fundamental analysis, technical analysis, or a blend of both, a thorough understanding of these approaches is crucial for evaluating investment opportunities and making informed decisions in the dynamic world of financial markets.

CHAPTER 9

Market Trends and Economic Factors

Introduction

Market trends and economic factors are intricately intertwined, shaping the landscape in which businesses operate and investors make decisions. Understanding market cycles and economic indicators is paramount for investors seeking to navigate the volatile terrain of financial markets. This essay delves into the concepts of market cycles, economic indicators, and their profound impact on investment decisions.

- **Understanding Market Cycles**

Market cycles encapsulate the natural rhythm of economic expansion and contraction. These cycles typically consist of four stages: expansion, peak, contraction, and trough. During the expansion phase, economic activity flourishes, marked by rising GDP, increased consumer spending, and high employment rates. Stock markets tend to perform well, and investors witness robust growth in their portfolios.

As the economy reaches its peak, signs of overheating become apparent. Inflationary pressures mount, leading central banks to tighten monetary policy to curb excessive growth. This tightening often precipitates a contraction phase. Consumer spending slows, businesses cut back on investments, and economic growth decelerates. Stock markets falter, and investors become cautious amid the impending downturn.

The contraction phase bottoms out at the trough, characterized by low consumer confidence, high unemployment, and diminished economic activity. However, it is during this phase that savvy investors often find opportunities, as assets may be undervalued. Eventually, the cycle restarts, and the economy begins its expansion phase anew.

- **Economic Indicators and their Impact on Investments**

Economic indicators are crucial metrics that provide insights into the health of an economy. They assist investors in assessing the current and future state of the economy, guiding their investment decisions. Several key indicators influence investment strategies:

Gross Domestic Product (GDP): GDP measures a country's economic output. Investors monitor GDP growth rates as they reflect the economy's overall health. Higher GDP growth often translates to increased corporate profits and, subsequently, higher stock prices.

Unemployment Rate: The unemployment rate indicates the percentage of the workforce without jobs. High unemployment rates may signal economic weakness, affecting consumer spending and investment sentiments. Conversely, low unemployment rates often coincide with economic growth.

Consumer Price Index (CPI): CPI measures the average change in prices consumers pay for goods and services. Inflationary pressures can erode purchasing power, impacting investment returns. Investors monitor CPI to gauge potential effects on interest rates and bond yields.

Interest Rates: Central banks set interest rates to manage economic growth and inflation. Changes in interest rates influence borrowing costs, corporate profitability, and stock market valuations. Rising rates may dampen investment enthusiasm, while lower rates can stimulate economic activity.

Stock Market Indices: Indices like the S&P 500 or Dow Jones Industrial Average serve as barometers of market sentiment. Movements in these indices reflect investors' collective outlook on economic conditions and corporate performance.

The impact of these indicators on investments can vary based on market conditions and investor perceptions. For instance, during periods of economic expansion, investors may favor riskier assets like stocks, aiming to capitalize on growth opportunities. Conversely, during economic contractions, investors often seek safer havens such as bonds or defensive stocks to protect their portfolios from market downturns.

Conclusion

Market trends and economic factors are pivotal in shaping investment strategies. Understanding market cycles and economic indicators enables investors to make informed decisions, mitigating risks and capitalizing on opportunities. By staying attuned to these factors and adapting to evolving market conditions, investors can navigate the dynamic landscape of financial markets more adeptly, optimizing their chances for long-term success.

In conclusion, market cycles and economic indicators serve as indispensable tools for investors, providing valuable insights that guide their investment decisions in an ever-changing economic landscape.

CHAPTER 10

Ethics and Social Responsibility in Investing

In recent years, the landscape of investing has experienced a transformative shift, with an increasing emphasis on ethical considerations and social responsibility. Investors, both individual and institutional, are recognizing the significance of incorporating ethical principles into their investment strategies. This evolution has given rise to responsible investment practices and impact investing, which are integral components of a broader movement toward aligning financial objectives with ethical, social, and environmental goals.

- **Responsible Investment Practices**

Responsible investment practices encompass a spectrum of approaches aimed at integrating environmental, social, and governance (ESG) factors into investment decisions. The fundamental premise revolves around the idea that financial success need not be at odds with social and environmental responsibility. Instead, it emphasizes the potential for investments to drive positive change while still generating profitable returns.

Environmental Considerations

Environmental factors have gained substantial traction in responsible investing. Investors are increasingly scrutinizing a company's impact on the environment, assessing its carbon footprint, resource usage, and commitment to sustainability. By favoring environmentally conscious companies, investors can channel capital toward businesses that prioritize renewable energy, waste reduction, and eco-friendly practices.

Social Factors

Social considerations encompass a broad array of criteria, such as labor standards, human rights, diversity, and community engagement. Investors are evaluating companies' treatment of employees, supply chain practices, and contributions to societal well-being. Investments are directed towards companies fostering inclusive workplaces, promoting fair labor practices, and supporting local communities through philanthropic initiatives.

Governance Practices

Governance criteria focus on a company's leadership, accountability, and transparency. Investors evaluate the effectiveness of corporate governance structures, assessing board independence, executive compensation, and adherence to ethical standards. Emphasis is placed on investing in companies with robust governance frameworks, reducing the risk of corporate malpractice and enhancing long-term sustainability.

- **Impact Investing**

While responsible investment practices consider ESG factors, impact investing takes it a step further by actively seeking measurable social or environmental impact alongside financial returns. Impact investors aim to generate positive outcomes by deploying capital into enterprises and projects that address pressing societal challenges.

Measurable Impact

The distinguishing feature of impact investing is its explicit focus on measurable outcomes. Investors target specific social or environmental objectives, whether it's mitigating climate change, promoting gender equality, or addressing healthcare disparities. Investments are assessed based on their tangible contributions toward achieving these objectives, creating a double bottom line of financial returns and societal impact.

Diverse Investment Vehicles

Impact investing spans various asset classes and investment vehicles. From private equity and venture capital to fixed income and public equity, impact investors have a diverse range of options to align their investment strategies with their values. Additionally, the emergence of specialized impact funds and social impact bonds offers investors specific avenues to target their desired impact areas.

Collaborative Partnerships

Impact investing often involves collaboration among investors, philanthropists, governments, and nonprofits. These partnerships leverage collective expertise and resources to tackle complex societal challenges. By fostering collaboration, impact investors amplify their ability to effect meaningful change and drive scalable solutions to pressing global issues.

The Evolution of Ethical Investment

The evolution of responsible investment practices and impact investing signifies a paradigm shift in the financial landscape. Traditionally, the sole focus of investing was maximizing financial returns, often disregarding the broader societal implications of investment decisions. However, with increased awareness and a growing sense of social responsibility, investors are acknowledging the interconnectedness between financial success and societal well-being.

Integration of Ethical Considerations

The integration of ethical considerations into investment strategies is not merely a trend; it reflects a fundamental revaluation of investment philosophies. Investors are recognizing that long-term financial success is intrinsically linked to environmental sustainability, social stability, and good governance practices. As such, ethical considerations are becoming an integral part of investment analysis and decision-making processes.

Shifting Investor Preferences

A significant driver behind the rise of ethical investing is the shifting preferences of investors. Millennials and Generation Z, in particular, place a premium on investing in alignment with their values. These cohorts prioritize investments that demonstrate a commitment to ESG principles and social impact, exerting influence on the investment landscape by driving demand for responsible investment options.

Regulatory and Institutional Support

Regulatory bodies and institutional investors are also playing a pivotal role in promoting responsible investment practices. Regulators are increasingly mandating greater transparency and disclosure of ESG-related information, enabling investors to make more informed decisions. Furthermore, institutional investors, including pension funds and endowments, are integrating ESG considerations into their investment policies, further reinforcing the importance of ethical investing.

Challenges and Future Outlook

Despite the remarkable progress, ethical investing faces several challenges that warrant attention for its continued growth and impact.

Measurement and Standardization

Measuring the impact of investments remains a challenge. Establishing standardized metrics and methodologies to assess social and environmental impact across diverse sectors and investment types is essential for credibility and comparability.

Balancing Financial Returns and Impact

A persistent concern for investors is the trade-off between financial returns and impact. Striking a balance between achieving competitive financial performance and generating meaningful societal or environmental impact poses a continual challenge.

Education and Awareness

Enhancing investor education and awareness about responsible investment practices is crucial. Many investors still lack a comprehensive understanding of ESG factors and impact investing, limiting the adoption of these strategies.

Scaling Impact

While impactful initiatives exist, scaling these solutions to address systemic challenges on a larger scale remains a hurdle. Mobilizing sufficient capital and resources to tackle global issues requires innovative approaches and collaboration across sectors.

Conclusion

Ethical considerations in investing, encompassing responsible investment practices and impact investing, represent a pivotal shift in the investment landscape. Investors are increasingly recognizing their role in driving positive change while seeking financial returns. By integrating ESG factors, targeting measurable impact, and aligning investments with ethical values, the evolution toward responsible and impactful investing is poised to continue reshaping the financial industry, fostering a more sustainable and inclusive global economy. As the momentum behind ethical investing grows, addressing challenges and fostering broader awareness will be integral in realizing its full potential and ensuring a more equitable and sustainable future.

In conclusion, the ethical evolution in investing, through responsible investment practices and impact investing, is transforming the investment landscape. These approaches not only seek financial returns but also emphasize positive social and environmental outcomes. By integrating ESG factors, measuring impact, and aligning investments with ethical values, the trend toward responsible and impactful investing is reshaping the financial industry for a more sustainable and inclusive global economy. As this momentum grows, addressing challenges and promoting awareness will be essential to realize the full potential of ethical investing, ensuring a more equitable and sustainable future.

CHAPTER 11

Tax planning and optimization

Tax planning and optimization are integral components of financial management that focus on minimizing tax liabilities while maximizing after-tax returns. They encompass a range of strategies and considerations aimed at legally reducing tax burdens, particularly concerning investments. Efficient tax planning not only helps in preserving wealth but also enhances the overall returns on investments. This article delves into tax-efficient investing strategies and underscores the significance of tax planning in investment decisions.

- **Tax-Efficient Investing Strategies**

1. Asset Location:

Asset location involves strategically placing different types of investments across various accounts to optimize tax efficiency. Assets generating higher taxable income, like bonds or actively managed funds, are ideally placed in tax-deferred accounts like IRAs or 401(k)s. In contrast, tax-efficient investments such as stocks are better suited for taxable brokerage accounts due to their lower tax impact.

2. Tax-Loss Harvesting:

This strategy involves selling investments that have experienced a loss to offset realized gains, thereby reducing the overall tax liability. Investors can use these losses to offset capital gains dollar for dollar and can even deduct up to $3,000 in excess losses against ordinary income.

3. Dividend Investing:

Investors can opt for qualified dividends that are taxed at preferential rates, offering tax advantages over interest income or non-qualified dividends. Dividend-paying stocks, especially those with a history of consistent and growing dividends, can be an integral part of a tax-efficient investment portfolio.

4. Long-Term Capital Gains:

Holding investments for the long term (over a year) qualifies for long-term capital gains tax rates, which are generally lower than short-term capital gains rates. This strategy incentivizes investors to maintain their positions for an extended period, reducing the tax impact upon selling appreciated assets.

5. Utilizing Tax-Advantaged Accounts:

Contributing to retirement accounts such as Traditional or Roth IRAs and 401(k)s allows investors to benefit from tax-deferred or tax-free growth, depending on the account type. Maximizing contributions to these accounts enables individuals to minimize current tax liabilities and build wealth over time.

- **Importance of Tax Planning in Investments**

1. Enhanced Returns:

Effective tax planning significantly impacts investment returns. By reducing the tax burden, investors can retain more of their gains, leading to higher overall returns. Over time, even seemingly small tax savings can compound into substantial wealth accumulation.

2. Risk Management:

Tax planning involves evaluating the tax implications of different investment decisions. It helps investors understand the potential tax consequences before making investment choices, contributing to better risk management and informed decision-making.

3. Long-Term Wealth Preservation:

Consistent tax planning ensures that investors retain more of their earnings, allowing for better capital preservation and wealth accumulation over the long term. By employing tax-efficient strategies, individuals can safeguard their financial resources for future needs and goals.

4. Compliance and Legal Obligations:

Proper tax planning ensures compliance with tax laws and regulations. Being aware of tax implications helps investors avoid potential penalties, audits, or legal issues, ensuring adherence to the tax code while optimizing tax efficiency.

5. Flexibility and Adaptability:

Tax planning provides investors with flexibility to adapt to changing financial circumstances, tax laws, or market conditions. Regularly reviewing and adjusting strategies based on evolving tax regulations and personal financial goals allows for optimal tax efficiency.

In conclusion, tax planning and optimization play pivotal roles in investment management, allowing investors to minimize tax liabilities and maximize after-tax returns. Implementing tax-efficient investing strategies, coupled with a thorough understanding of the importance of tax planning in investments, can significantly impact financial success and long-term wealth accumulation. By strategically navigating the tax landscape, investors can achieve their financial objectives while minimizing the erosion of their investment returns due to taxes.

CHAPTER 12

Retirement Planning

Retirement planning is a crucial aspect of financial management that involves setting goals and strategies to ensure financial security during one's retirement years. It's a process that evolves throughout a person's life and demands a proactive approach to achieve a comfortable and financially stable retirement. In this article, we will explore the fundamental aspects of creating a retirement plan and strategies for securing a stable future.

- **Creating a Retirement Plan**

a. Assessing Current Financial Situation

The first step in crafting a retirement plan involves assessing one's current financial situation. It includes evaluating income, expenses, assets, debts, and existing retirement accounts. Understanding these factors lays the groundwork for establishing retirement goals.

b. Setting Retirement Goals

Setting realistic and achievable retirement goals is crucial. Factors to consider include the desired retirement age, expected lifestyle, estimated expenses, healthcare costs, travel aspirations, and other activities that one plans to pursue during retirement.

c. Estimating Retirement Expenses

Estimating future expenses is essential for creating an effective retirement plan. This includes considering housing, healthcare, utilities, transportation, leisure activities, and potential emergencies. Creating a detailed budget helps in projecting how much savings will be required to maintain the desired lifestyle.

d. Retirement Savings Vehicles

Several retirement savings vehicles are available, such as employer-sponsored retirement plans (e.g., 401(k)), Individual Retirement Accounts (IRAs), annuities, and taxable investment accounts. Each has its benefits and tax implications. Diversifying across these vehicles can provide a robust retirement portfolio.

e. Implementing a Savings Strategy

Regularly contributing to retirement accounts is crucial. Taking advantage of employer matches, maximizing contributions, and utilizing catch-up contributions for those nearing retirement age are effective strategies. It's essential to start early to benefit from compounding interest.

f. Managing Investments

Asset allocation is key in managing retirement investments. Balancing risk and return based on one's risk tolerance and time horizon is critical. As retirement approaches, shifting to a more conservative investment strategy to protect savings becomes prudent.

g. Contingency Planning

Preparing for unforeseen circumstances is vital. Creating an emergency fund and having insurance coverage, including health insurance and long-term care insurance, can protect retirement savings from unexpected expenses.

- **Strategies for a Secure Retirement**

a. Start Early and Consistently Save

Time is a valuable asset when it comes to retirement savings. Starting early allows for more extended periods of compound growth. Even small, consistent contributions over time can accumulate significantly.

b. Take Advantage of Employer Benefits

Many employers offer retirement benefits like 401(k) matching contributions. Taking full advantage of these benefits maximizes savings potential. Contribute at least enough to meet the employer's match to leverage free money for retirement.

c. Diversify Investments

Diversification spreads risk across different asset classes, reducing the impact of market fluctuations. A well-diversified portfolio can include stocks, bonds, mutual funds, and other investment vehicles.

d. Consider Health Care Costs

Healthcare expenses tend to rise in retirement. Understanding Medicare options, investing in health savings accounts (HSAs), and considering long-term care insurance can mitigate potential healthcare-related financial burdens.

e. Plan for a Long Retirement

Increased life expectancy means retirees may spend more years in retirement than previous generations. Planning for a longer retirement period ensures savings last throughout one's life.

f. Monitor and Adjust the Plan

Life circumstances change, as do financial markets. Regularly reviewing and adjusting the retirement plan ensures it stays aligned with goals and accounts for any changes in income, expenses, or market conditions.

g. Seek Professional Advice

Consulting a financial advisor can provide valuable insights and guidance tailored to individual circumstances. They can help navigate complex financial decisions and optimize retirement strategies.

In conclusion, retirement planning is a continuous process that involves careful consideration of current financial status, setting realistic goals, diligent savings, and prudent investment management. Implementing these strategies can significantly contribute to a secure and comfortable retirement. Starting early, being informed, and regularly reassessing the plan are vital steps toward achieving financial independence in retirement.

CHAPTER 13

Adapting to Changing Financial Landscapes

In a world characterized by constant flux, the financial landscape is no exception. It's a dynamic ecosystem shaped by various factors, from geopolitical events to technological advancements. Two crucial aspects in navigating this ever-evolving terrain include understanding and navigating market volatility and embracing technological changes in investing.

- **Navigating Market Volatility**

Market volatility refers to the rapid and unpredictable price fluctuations experienced by financial markets. It's influenced by numerous elements, including economic indicators, political instability, global events, and even human psychology. Navigating this volatility is essential for investors, as it can create both risks and opportunities.

Understanding Volatility

Volatility isn't inherently negative; it's an inherent aspect of financial markets. Understanding its nature can assist investors in making informed decisions. Tools like the Volatility Index (VIX) help gauge market expectations for volatility and are instrumental in devising risk management strategies.

Diversification and Risk Management

One effective approach to mitigate the impact of market volatility is through diversification. Allocating investments across various asset classes can help spread risk. Additionally, employing risk management techniques like stop-loss orders or options contracts can limit potential losses during turbulent market periods.

Long-Term Perspective

Maintaining a long-term perspective amid volatility is crucial. Market fluctuations are often short-term in nature and may not reflect the intrinsic value of investments. Patiently weathering market storms has historically rewarded investors who remain focused on their long-term financial goals.

Importance of Research and Education

Education and research are potent tools for investors. Staying informed about market trends, economic indicators, and global events equips individuals with the knowledge needed to make sound investment decisions. Continuous learning helps adapt strategies to changing market conditions.

Role of Professional Advice

Seeking advice from financial advisors or professionals can provide invaluable insights. They can offer guidance tailored to individual financial goals, risk tolerance, and market conditions, aiding in making informed decisions amidst market volatility.

- **Embracing Technological Changes in Investing**

Technology has revolutionized the investment landscape, significantly altering how individuals access and interact with financial markets.

Rise of Robo-Advisors and AI

Robo-advisors, powered by artificial intelligence (AI), have gained prominence. These automated platforms offer algorithm-driven portfolio management, making investing more accessible and cost-effective for retail investors. AI-driven analysis can swiftly process vast amounts of data, providing insights and enhancing investment decisions.

Fintech Innovations

Fintech innovations have democratized finance, introducing platforms for crowdfunding, peer-to-peer lending, and mobile payments. Blockchain technology, particularly in cryptocurrencies, has disrupted traditional financial systems, offering decentralized and transparent transaction networks.

Access to Global Markets

Technology has removed barriers to entry into global markets. Online trading platforms enable individuals to invest in international stocks, currencies, and commodities with ease. This increased access has diversified portfolios and provided exposure to previously inaccessible markets.

Data Analytics and Predictive Tools

Data analytics tools enable investors to analyze market trends, predict patterns, and make informed decisions. Machine learning algorithms sift through vast datasets, identifying potential investment opportunities and aiding in risk assessment.

Cybersecurity Challenges

As technology advances, cybersecurity becomes a paramount concern. Safeguarding personal and financial information from cyber threats is crucial. Investors and financial institutions must prioritize robust security measures to protect against potential breaches.

Conclusion

Adapting to changing financial landscapes necessitates a proactive approach. Navigating market volatility demands a combination of strategic planning, risk management, education, and a long-term perspective. Embracing technological changes in investing involves leveraging advancements to optimize investment strategies while being mindful of potential risks like cybersecurity threats.

In this fast-evolving financial world, flexibility, continuous learning, and a willingness to embrace innovation are key. By understanding market volatility and leveraging technological advancements, investors can better navigate the unpredictable currents of the financial landscape and position themselves for long-term success.

CONCLUSION

The money-minded investor embodies a complex persona shaped by a multitude of factors ranging from personal aspirations to economic circumstances. This archetype is characterized by a sharp focus on financial gain, often prioritizing wealth accumulation and profit maximization above other considerations. Within the diverse landscape of investors, this mindset plays a pivotal role, influencing investment decisions, risk tolerance, and overall financial strategy.

At the core of the money-minded investor's approach lies a deep-seated pursuit of monetary success. Whether driven by a desire for financial security, achieving specific life goals, or attaining a certain standard of living, this investor type meticulously navigates the world of finance with a single-minded dedication to increasing wealth. The pursuit of financial gain becomes a guiding principle that directs their investment choices, leading to a diverse portfolio tailored to generate profits and secure returns.

One of the defining traits of the money-minded investor is their keen awareness of market trends, economic indicators, and investment opportunities. They meticulously research potential investments, staying informed about industry developments, economic forecasts, and market fluctuations. This knowledge empowers them to make informed decisions, seizing opportunities for growth and mitigating risks.

Risk assessment is an integral aspect of the money-minded investor's strategy. While driven by profit, they are not reckless; instead, they calculate risks meticulously. This approach often involves a balanced portfolio, diversification across asset classes, and a calculated allocation of resources to minimize potential losses while maximizing gains. However, the constant pursuit of higher returns can lead to a higher risk appetite, occasionally exposing them to volatile markets or speculative ventures.

The money-minded investor's mindset extends beyond personal finance; it influences broader economic dynamics. Their investments can stimulate economic growth, fund innovation, and creat employment opportunities. They contribute to capital formation, aiding in the expansion of businesses and facilitating economic development. Consequently, they hold a significant role in shaping the financial landscape, affecting industries, markets, and even government policies.

However, the exclusive focus on monetary gains can have drawbacks. Tunnel vision towards profits may overshadow ethical considerations or the broader societal impact of investments. Ethical dilemmas regarding investments in industries that may harm the environment or exploit labor can arise, challenging the moral compass of the money-minded investor. Balancing financial gain with ethical responsibility becomes a critical aspect that demands attention in their investment decisions.

Moreover, the incessant pursuit of wealth might lead to a neglect of non-financial aspects of life, impacting personal relationships, health, and overall well-being. The relentless pursuit of financial success may result in stress, anxiety, or burnout, creating a trade-off between financial accomplishments and personal fulfillment.

In an evolving financial landscape, the money-minded investor must adapt to changing paradigms. Technological advancements, geopolitical shifts, and socio-economic changes constantly redefine investment opportunities and risks. Embracing innovation, understanding emerging markets, and navigating digital disruptions become essential for continued success.

As financial markets continue to globalize and diversify, the money-minded investor faces both challenges and opportunities. Cultural differences, regulatory variations, and geopolitical tensions impact investment strategies and risk assessments. Adapting to these diverse landscapes while maintaining a sharp focus on financial objectives necessitates a nuanced and flexible approach.

In conclusion, the money-minded investor epitomizes a multifaceted persona deeply entrenched in the pursuit of financial prosperity. Their meticulous approach, market awareness, and risk management strategies define their investment style, influencing both personal financial growth and broader economic dynamics. However, the quest for monetary success requires a delicate balance with ethical considerations and personal well-being. Adapting to evolving financial landscapes while remaining vigilant to opportunities and risks will be crucial for the money-minded investor to thrive in a dynamic and ever-changing financial world.

Appendix

Glossary of Investment Terms

Asset Allocation: The strategy of dividing a portfolio among different asset classes (such as stocks, bonds, and cash) to manage risk and achieve specific investment goals.

Diversification: Spreading investments across various assets to reduce risk. It involves investing in different sectors, industries, or geographic regions.

ETF (Exchange-Traded Fund): A type of investment fund that holds assets such as stocks, commodities, or bonds. ETFs are traded on stock exchanges and offer diversified exposure to a particular market.

Index Fund: A mutual fund or ETF designed to track the performance of a specific index (e.g S&P 500). They aim to replicate the holdings and performance of the index they track.

Liquidity: The ease with which an asset can be bought or sold in the market without causing significant price changes. Cash is considered the most liquid asset.

Portfolio: A collection of financial investments owned by an individual or an entity. It can consist of stocks, bonds, mutual funds, ETFs, and other securities.

Risk Tolerance: An investor's ability to endure fluctuations in the value of their investments. I determines the level of risk an investor is comfortable taking.

Volatility: A measure of the variation in the price of a financial instrument over time. High volatility indicates greater price fluctuations, which can signify higher risk.

Yield: The income return on an investment, usually in the form of interest or dividends, expressed as a percentage of the investment's cost.

Additional Resources for Further Reading

- *Books:*

    - "The Intelligent Investor" by Benjamin Graham

    - "A Random Walk Down Wall Street" by Burton Malkiel

    - "Common Stocks and Uncommon Profits" by Philip Fisher

- *Websites and Online Resources:*

    - Investopedia (www.investopedia.com): Offers comprehensive articles, tutorials, and educational content on various investment topics.

    - Morningstar (www.morningstar.com): Provides investment research, analysis, and tools for investors.

    - Financial Times (www.ft.com): Offers news, analysis, and commentary on financial markets and investments.

- *Courses and Seminars:*

    - Coursera (www.coursera.org) and Udemy (www.udemy.com): Offer online courses on investment strategies, finance, and stock market analysis.

    - Local investment clubs or workshops often organize seminars and discussions on investing.